TRIANGLE HISTORIES
★★★★ ★ ★★★★
THE CIVIL WAR

JEFFERSON DAVIS

W. Scott Ingram

BLACKBIRCH PRESS

THOMSON
———— ✳ ————
GALE

Detroit • New York • San Diego • San Francisco
Boston • New Haven, Conn. • Waterville, Maine
London • Munich

Published by Blackbirch Press
10911 Technology Place
San Diego, CA 92127
Web site: http://www.galegroup.com/blackbirch
e-mail: customerservice@galegroup.com

Printed in China

10 9 8 7 6 5 4 3 2 1

Photo credits:
Cover, back cover, pages 28-29, 32, 36, 38, 47, 51, 63, 66, 72, 73, 75 ©
North Wind Picture Archives; Cover, pages 12, 23, 26, 31, 39, 41, 46, 50,
53, 70, 80 © Dover Publications; pages 9, 10, 13, 18, 21, 25, 44-45, 56, 64,
77 © Library of Congress; pages 27, 62 © CORBIS; page 33 © Alabama
Bureau of Tourism and Travel; page 49 © Unites States Senate Historical
Office; page 64 © King Visual Technology; page 65 © Hulton/Archive;
page 68 © University of North Carolina, Library at Chapel Hill; page 78
© National Archive; page 99 © The Museum of the Confederacy, Richmond,
Virginia, Copy Photography by Katherine Wetzel

Library of Congress Cataloging-in-Publication Data
Ingram, Scott (William Scott)
Jefferson Davis / by W. Scott Ingram.
        p. cm. — (The Civil War)
Includes index.
Summary: Traces the life of Jefferson Davis, who graduated from West Point
and served in the Army and the House of Representatives before becoming
President of the Confederate States of America during the Civil War.
        ISBN 1-56711-565-9 (hardcover : alk. paper)
1. Davis, Jefferson, 1808-1889—Juvenile literature. 2. Presidents—
Confederate States of America—Biography—Juvenile literature. 3.
Statesmen—United States—Biography—Juvenile literature. [1. Davis,
Jefferson, 1808-1889. 2. Presidents-Confederate States of America. 3.
Confederate States of America.] I. Title. II. Civil War (San Diego, California)
E467.1.D26 154 2002
973.7'13'092-dc21   2001006245

CONTENTS

PREFACE: THE CIVIL WAR

Nearly 150 years after the final shots were fired, the Civil War remains one of the key events in U. S. history. The enormous loss of life alone makes it tragically unique: More Americans died in Civil War battles than in all other American wars combined. More Americans fell at the Battle of Gettysburg than during any battle in American military history. And, in one day at the Battle of Antietam, more Americans were killed and wounded than in any other day in American history.

Slaves did the backbreaking work on Southern plantations.

As tragic as the loss of life was, however, it is the principles over which the war was fought that make it uniquely American. Those beliefs—equality and freedom—are the foundation of American democracy, our basic rights. It was the bitter disagreement about the exact nature of those rights that drove our nation to its bloodiest war.

The disagreements grew in part from the differing economies of the North and South. The warm climate and wide-open areas of the Southern states were ideal for an economy based on agriculture. In the first half of the 19th century, the main cash crop was cotton, grown on large farms called plantations. Slaves, who were brought to the United States from Africa, were forced to do the backbreaking work of planting and harvesting cotton. They also provided the other labor necessary to keep plantations running. Slaves were bought and sold like property, and had been critical to the Southern economy since the first Africans came to America in 1619.

The suffering of African Americans under slavery is one of the great tragedies in American history. And the debate over whether the United States government had the right to forbid slavery—in both Southern states and in new territories—was a dispute that overshadowed the first 80 years of our history.

For many Northerners, the question of slavery was one of morality and not economics. Because the Northern economy was based on manufacturing rather than agriculture, there was little need for slave labor. The primary economic need of Northern states was a protective tax known as a tariff that would make imported goods more expensive than goods made in the North. Tariffs forced Southerners to buy Northern goods and made them economically dependent on the North, a fact that led to deep resentment among Southerners.

Economic control did not matter to the anti-slavery Northerners known as abolitionists. Their conflict with the South was over slavery. The idea that the federal government could outlaw slavery was perfectly reasonable. After all, abolitionists contended, our nation was founded on the idea that all people are created equal. How could slavery exist in such a country?

For the Southern states that joined the Confederacy, the freedom from unfair taxation and the right to make their

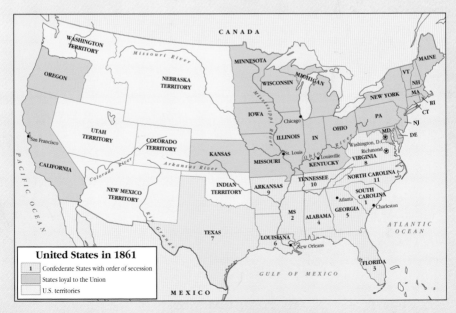

United States in 1861
- 1   Confederate States with order of secession
- States loyal to the Union
- U.S. territories

own decisions about slavery was as important a principle as equality. For most Southerners, the right of states to decide what is best for its citizens was the most important principle guaranteed in the Constitution.

The conflict over these principles generated sparks throughout the decades leading up to the Civil War. The importance of keeping an equal number of slave and free states in the Union became critical to Southern lawmakers in Congress in those years. In 1820, when Maine and Missouri sought admission to the Union, the question was settled by the Missouri Compromise: Maine was admitted as a free state, Missouri as a slave state, thus maintaining a balance in Congress. The compromise stated that all future territories north of the southern boundary of Missouri would enter the Union as free states, those south of it would be slave states.

In 1854, however, the Kansas-Nebraska Act set the stage for the Civil War. That act repealed the Missouri Compromise and by declaring that the question of slavery should be decided by residents of the territory, set off a rush of pro- and anti-slavery settlers to the new land. Violence between the two sides began almost immediately and soon "Bleeding Kansas" became a tragic chapter in our nation's story.

With Lincoln's election on an anti-slavery platform in 1860, the disagreement over the power of the federal government reached its breaking point. In early 1861, South Carolina became the first state to secede from the Union, followed by Mississippi, Florida, Alabama, Georgia, Louisiana, Virginia, Texas, North Carolina, Tennessee, and Arkansas. Those eleven states became the Confederate States of America. Confederate troops fired the first shots of the Civil War at Fort Sumter, South Carolina, on April 12, 1861. Those shots began a four-year war in which thousands of Americans—Northerners and Southerners—would give, in President Lincoln's words, "the last full measure of devotion."

OPPOSITE: The Confederate attack on Fort Sumter began the Civil War.

Introduction: "He Threw Off the Cloak with Defiance"

By early April 1865, the Civil War was in its final terrible weeks and Union forces had taken control of Richmond, the Confederate capital. Though Jefferson Davis, the president of the Confederacy, had fled Richmond, he was still in office. His home, and that of the entire Confederate government, was now a twelve-car railroad train. Even as Robert E. Lee and his Army of Northern Virginia surrendered to Union general Ulysses S. Grant on April 9, the "government on wheels" rolled south. Davis had not given up hope of a Confederate victory.

By mid-April, Davis's train had come to the end of usable track. His party continued south on horseback, escorted by a cavalry unit. As he traveled, his advisors and cabinet gave up and fell by the wayside. But Davis; his wife, Varina; and the Rebel horsemen continued to ride more than 300 miles through the South.

On May 3, Davis and his guards crossed into Georgia. By that time, there was a reward of $100,000 for his capture. Union lawmakers had accused him of planning the assassination of Lincoln, which had occurred two weeks earlier. Thus he was not just a fugitive leader—he was a man with a price on head. Union troops on his

Union troops captured Jefferson Davis on May 10, 1865. Davis tried to escape while wearing a woman's shawl and cloak.

trail pursued him that much harder, eager to win a possible bounty.

On May 10, Davis could flee no farther. During the night, Union cavalry had surrounded his camp and his escorts. Varina Davis gave her husband her cloak and shawl and sent him into the brush to hide.

But there was no escape. President Jefferson Davis was trapped. In later years, Varina Davis wrote that when cornered, her husband "threw off the cloak in defiance."

On that morning, however, Jefferson Davis, a war hero, former senator, and secretary of war, was taunted mercilessly by Union soldiers. He had been captured while dressed in women's clothes.

9

Chapter 1

FROM LOG CABIN TO PLANTATION

In the dramatic American story that is the Civil War, many names stand out. Abraham Lincoln, Ulysses S. Grant, William Sherman, Robert E. Lee, and "Stonewall" Jackson are among the many people recognized for their great contributions, whether they fought for the North or the South. One man, Jefferson Davis, is often overlooked in the history of that tragic period. Nevertheless, the president of the Confederacy belongs with those who achieved greatness during that terrible time.

OPPOSITE: Jefferson Davis posed for this picture several years after the Civil War.

11

Jefferson Davis was named after U.S. president Thomas Jefferson (above).

Jefferson Davis was born on June 3, 1808, in a log cabin near Fairview, Kentucky. Abraham Lincoln, coincidentally, was born eight months later in a log cabin less than ten miles away.

Jefferson was the youngest of ten children. His father, Samuel Davis, named his son after the president then in office, Thomas Jefferson of Virginia. (Some scholars believe the boy also had a middle name, Finis, French for "finished," which his parents gave him to indicate that they did not plan to have any more children. The oldest child in the family, Joseph, was twenty-three years older than Jefferson.)

The Davis family did not remain in Kentucky after the birth of their youngest child. The farm there was too small to produce enough food for the large Davis family. In 1811, when Jefferson was three years old, the family settled in Woodville, a small farming village in the territory of Mississippi. There they bought a large amount of land and built a farm they called Rosemont.

Samuel Davis believed that the key to a successful life was a good education. In the early 1800s, however, there were no free public schools. Therefore, young Jefferson and his sister

The Davis family moved from Kentucky to this home in Woodville, Mississippi.

Mary Ellen were taught the basics of reading and writing by their older brother Benjamin.

In 1816, Mr. and Mrs. Davis sent Jefferson, age 8, to a private religious school several hundred miles away in Springfield, Kentucky. After two years, Jefferson returned to Rosemont, traveling down the Mississippi River in one of the first steamboats to run on the great river. By the time Jefferson returned home, Mississippi had entered the Union as the twentieth state.

Jefferson was sent to a small private school closer to home. But he was not interested in his studies and often talked back to his teachers. One day, the twelve-year-old Jefferson decided that he was going to quit school. He told his father of his decision.

13

Samuel Davis replied that his son he could quit if he wanted to, but he had to make himself useful. Jefferson was put to work picking cotton under the blazing Mississippi sun. Two days later, he was back in school.

A National Debate

While young Jefferson Davis was making decisions about his future, lawmakers in the U.S. Congress were making decisions about the future of the young country. The United States was growing quickly, and many new territories wanted to enter the Union. The problem was that some of these territories allowed slavery, and some prohibited it. In 1820, the question of whether to allow a territory to enter the Union as a slave or free state divided the country.

A year earlier, the territory of Missouri had asked to be admitted to the Union. Slavery was permitted in Missouri Territory. But Northern abolitionists— those opposed to slavery—had no intention of letting it remain so. They insisted that their representatives deny Missouri's statehood. When Missouri's statehood bill was brought before the House of Representatives, New York Congressman James Talmadge proposed an amendment restricting slavery within its borders.

Southern lawmakers were shocked by the Talmadge amendment. They had been unaware of the strong opposition to new slave states in

14

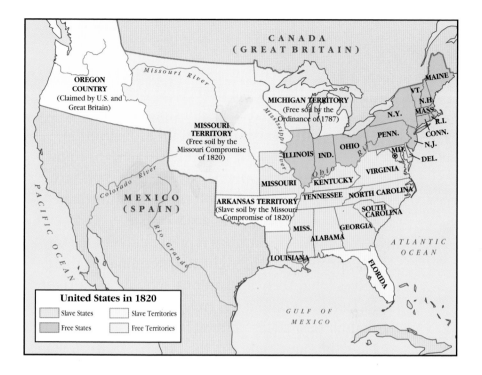

United States in 1820

Slave States
Free States
Slave Territories
Free Territories

Congress. What Southern legislators had overlooked was that there were now 11 free states and 11 slave states. Until that point, there had been a balance in admitting states. Slaveholding states Alabama and Mississippi had been balanced by free states Indiana and Illinois. Admitting Missouri as either free or slave would shift the balance in Congress.

The debates in Congress over slavery revealed for the first time how divided the two regions of the nation had become. The North saw no injustice in the proposed amendment to restrict slavery. Southern lawmakers, however, saw Missouri as one of their own—an agricultural region populated by Southerners and slaves. Thus, the Talmadge amendment was a threat to their way of life.

15

Town meetings were held across America to discuss the proposals. Northerners denounced the extension of slavery. Southerners invoked the Constitution, saying that it guaranteed the right to own property—that is, slaves. Five Northern states passed resolutions that protested Missouri's admission as a slave state.

Meanwhile, Southern representatives argued that people had the right to determine for themselves what their institutions should be—a right known as "popular sovereignty." They insisted that all new states coming into the Union should have the same rights as the original thirteen states to choose or reject slavery.

After many weeks of debate, Congress passed legislation that came to be known as the Missouri Compromise. In early 1820, the House passed a bill to admit Maine to the Union as a free state. When the bill was sent to the Senate, the Missouri petition for statehood was attached to it. Under the compromise, slavery would be allowed in Missouri but prohibited in any future states north of the line formed by Missouri's southern border.

Admitting Maine as a free state and Missouri as a slave state preserved the Senate balance between free and slave states. However, the question of how this balance would be maintained in the future was unsettled.

The Missouri Compromise was the most important single issue Congress had been forced to deal with until that time. Its passage also marked the beginning of the final forty years of debate over slavery, a practice that had been part of the American way of life for more than 200 years.

For Jefferson and the rest of the Davis family, slave ownership was considered necessary to operate a successful farm. Unfortunately for the Davises, a series of crop failures in 1821 hurt the family finances. They were forced to sell some of their slaves, and Samuel Davis could no longer afford to send Jefferson to school.

By this point in his life, Jefferson, like his parents, understood the importance of a good education. He decided to ask his oldest brother, Joseph, to pay for his schooling. Joseph, who had bought a plantation after a successful career as a lawyer, agreed. He was wealthy enough to pay for his little brother's education and had no children of his own to support. Thus, in 1821, Jefferson entered boarding school in Lexington, Kentucky.

For two years, Jefferson studied history, math, philosophy, and religion. He also learned to speak French. Once he graduated, he planned to attend the University of Virginia, the college founded by his namesake, Thomas Jefferson. He hoped to become a lawyer and planter like his brother.

Joseph Davis, however, had other plans for him. In 1823, Jefferson was shocked to learn that Joseph had obtained an appointment for him to attend the United States Military Academy in West Point, New York. For the first time in his life, Jefferson would be traveling to the North.

17

Chapter 2

FROM CADET TO CONGRESSMAN

Joseph Davis thought his younger brother would be excited by the news that he had been appointed to the U.S. Military Academy. Although the college was only twenty years old, it was already considered one of the finest schools in the country. There were thirty applicants for every opening.

OPPOSITE: Jefferson Davis attended the U.S. Military Academy at West Point, New York, shown here in the early 1800s.

Jefferson, however, was far from happy. He didn't want to travel so far from home—especially to the North. He had no interest in pursuing a military career either. Finally, Jefferson accepted the appointment when his family agreed that he could leave after one year if he decided that the school was not to his liking.

After that first year, however, Jefferson decided to remain at West Point. He actually enjoyed it a little too much, and got into trouble for "long hair," "messy room," an excessive amount of drinking, and other violations of the West Point rules. His classroom performance was not strong, either. Though he received good grades in French and drawing, Jefferson did poorly in mathematics and often did not turn in homework assignments. It is not surprising that he graduated near the bottom of his class in 1828.

An Officer on the Frontier

For the next several years, Second Lieutenant Jefferson Davis was stationed at outposts in the upper Mississippi River areas of Illinois and Wisconsin. Davis disliked almost everything about the first years of his military career. The snowy winters were bitterly cold, and the distance from home made visits impossible.

The worst part of Davis's early career, however, was the boredom. Very little was asked of the soldiers in these territories. Davis oversaw lumber operations and supervised the construction of forts. The only fighting in which he was involved was with Native Americans in the region.

Davis disliked ordering his troops to battle the Native Americans. He admired their culture, their courage, and their fighting ability. In several instances, Davis objected to the treatment of Native Americans by white settlers and the local militia.

Jefferson Davis, though not fond of military life, was respected by the men he commanded.

Although he was not fond of military life, Davis was liked and respected by the men under his command. He was calm and brave under pressure, and a fellow officer described Davis as "one of the most promising officers in the Army."

Davis, however, soon realized that a military career was not for him. The country was at peace, so there was little chance for advancement. The pay was low—less than $300 a year.

Most importantly, he had fallen in love with Sarah Knox Taylor, daughter of his commanding officer and future U.S. president, Colonel Zachary Taylor. And Taylor did not want his daughter to marry a soldier. He knew how rootless and dangerous the life of a military wife could be.

21

The Black Hawk War

Jefferson Davis's misgivings about the treatment of Native Americans grew especially intense during the Black Hawk War of 1832. This brief but violent episode in the history between the United States and Native American tribes began in the spring of 1832, when a group of Sauk Indians crossed the Mississippi River from Iowa to northern Illinois. The group, under the leadership of 65-year-old Chief Black Hawk, was seeking the right to return to their tribal lands near the junction of the Rock River and the Mississippi. The Sauk contended that the land had been taken from them through an illegal treaty.

White settlers on the land claimed by the Sauk panicked at the arrival of Black Hawk's band. Shooting broke out, with few casualties on either side. The fighting, however, drew both the Illinois State militia and the U.S. Army to the area. Upon learning of the arrival of the white troops, Black Hawk sent several of his men under a white flag to tell the soldiers that his band was returning across the Mississippi. Untrained militiamen shot and killed those men, however, as well as two others who arrived to check up on their companions.

Black Hawk

To retaliate, the Sauk attacked a village in southern Wisconsin and killed fifteen men, women, and children. The final and worst conflict of the war came in late summer 1832, when American troops massacred more than 400 Sauk men, women, and children at Fox River, Wisconsin.

Black Hawk was captured in this final fight and sent down the river to prison in St. Louis. One officer who accompanied the elderly chief was Lieutenant Jefferson Davis. Years later, Davis wrote of the war, "the real heroes were Black Hawk and his braves."

The Black Hawk War is notable for the involvement of three future presidents. Abraham Lincoln was a 23-year-old militia member (although he saw no action during the war). Colonel Zachary Taylor was a U.S. cavalry commander. And Jefferson Davis was a disillusioned young officer.

Thus, Davis resigned from active duty in 1835 after seven years in the army, and on June 17, 1835, he and "Knox" Taylor were married. The couple moved to Mississippi, where Davis planned to take over the operation of Brierfield, his brother Joseph's plantation. Joseph, nearing 60, had moved to a small house on the land and wanted to turn the plantation over to his younger brother. The situation seemed ideal until misfortune struck.

Both Davis and his wife came down with malaria a few months after arriving at Brierfield. Today, doctors know malaria is a disease caused by a parasite that is passed into humans through the bite of the anopheles mosquito. In Davis's time, it was believed that malaria—French for "bad air"—was caused by breathing humid air. The disease causes fever, chills, and sweating that, in some cases, can recur for years. In other cases, malaria can kill. Sarah Knox Taylor died only three months after her marriage to Davis.

A Quiet Decade

The death of his wife was heartbreaking for Davis. He spent the next eight years at Brierfield, living alone in the large main house and spending hours reading in the library at his brother Joseph's cottage. Davis's main companions on his plantation were his slaves. By that time, the state of Mississippi had one of largest slave populations of any state.

Slaves work on a tobacco plantation in the early 1800s.

Today, the word slavery brings to mind huge cotton plantations in Deep South states such as Mississippi. For most of the history of slavery in the United States, however, the area surrounding the Chesapeake Bay—Maryland, Delaware, and Virginia—was the place in which slavery had the strongest hold. The first slaves had arrived in the region to work on tobacco farms in 1619, and within a few decades slavery had become a way of life. In 1820, the year of the Missouri Compromise, almost two-thirds of the slaves in the United States lived in the farmland around the Chesapeake Bay.

Large farms arose in this area because the enormous Chesapeake Bay had many ideal ports for shipping goods abroad—and for bringing in slaves. In addition, most Native American tribes had been eliminated from the region, and it was a perfect area for raising tobacco and wheat. The labor of black slaves was the foundation of this economic system.

Andrew Jackson believed Native Americans should be removed from their traditional lands to make room for whites.

That economic system expanded with the introduction of the cotton plant and the cotton gin for cleaning the plant's fibers. By the 1830s, when Davis was establishing his plantation at Brierfield, cotton plantations were being built in Southern states, such as Alabama and Mississippi, that had ideal conditions for raising cotton.

The spread of the plantations was slowed, however, by the presence of Native Americans. Removing the tribes that had lived in the South for thousands of years became the mission of the federal government. And a man who

The Cherokee were forced to travel from the South to present-day Oklahoma in a journey that came to be called the "Trail of Tears."

believed Indian removal was a patriotic duty led the government.

From the late 1820s until the mid-1830s, the president was Andrew Jackson of Tennessee—a man Davis, and most Southerners, greatly admired. Jackson firmly believed in the right of Americans to migrate across the Appalachian Mountains, west to the Mississippi River and on across the continent, to settle wherever they pleased.

To Jackson—and many citizens who supported him—Native Americans were savages who belonged somewhere else. Throughout his term in office, Jackson used every means possible—both legal and illegal—to oust Native Americans from their traditional lands in the Midwest and South and force them to the plains of what are today Oklahoma, Kansas, and Nebraska.

27

The policy of Indian removal gradually opened enormous areas of land for white settlers. As Native Americans moved west of the Mississippi River, white planters and their slaves moved south into the lands they had left. Wealthy Southerners from the Atlantic coast built plantations in the new land. And where wealthy Southerners went, slaves went too. The dark, fertile soil and hot climate were ideal for a cotton industry that ran on slave labor.

In 1830, there were about 2 million slaves in the South, worth about $1 billion to their owners. Most were situated in the Chesapeake Bay region. Huge numbers of these slaves were taken to the blistering heat and brutal conditions of the Deep

Slaves performed the exhausting work of picking, baling, and ginning cotton.

South. Between 1830 and 1840, for example, the slave population of Mississippi alone grew by 200%. Slave labor made Mississippi the fifth wealthiest state in the Union by the beginning of the Civil War.

Many masters throughout the South brutally mistreated their slaves, but Davis did not. Though he was firm believer in the institution of slavery, he was unfailingly kind to his slaves. Davis's treatment of his slaves was so unusual that other plantation owners claimed the slaves at Brierfield were spoiled. "We had good grub, good clothes, and nobody worked hard," said one slave at Brierfield. Davis would not allow families of slaves to be broken up and sold. He even provided

29

health care and shelter for sick or elderly slaves.

Davis also refused to allow his slaves to be whipped. When a Brierfield slave broke the rules, a jury of slaves decided the punishment. Davis only insisted that he be able to change a punishment that he felt was too severe.

Many slaveholders hired white men, who often used cruel tactics, to supervise their slaves. Davis, however, had an African American named Jim Pemberton as his overseer. Pemberton, who had belonged to Samuel Davis, had nursed Davis back to health after his terrible episode with malaria, and Davis was tremendously grateful. He treated Pemberton like a friend, and two often sat on Davis's porch sharing brandy and cigars in the evening.

Davis was so isolated at Brierfield that he truly believed all slaves everywhere were treated as well as his slaves were. Thus the idea of passing federal laws to abolish slavery infuriated him. Like most Southern whites, he believed that the U.S. Constitution guaranteed him the right to own such human "property."

Davis's isolation had another result as well. As the years after Knox Taylor's death passed, Joseph Davis began to worry about his lonely brother, a widower at thirty-five. Finally, in 1843, he arranged for Davis to meet Varina Howell, the daughter of a planter in Natchez, Mississippi.

Though she was only 17, this tall, well-educated young woman won Davis's heart. Howell, in turn, was impressed with the older man. Few men in the South at that time had Davis's level of education and culture. In February 1845, the two were married, and Davis emerged from his lonely life at Brierfield.

Varina Howell married Jefferson Davis in 1845.

Now a successful and wealthy planter as well as an army veteran, Jefferson Davis made an ideal candidate for political office. In November 1845, he was elected to the U.S. House of Representatives and journeyed with his wife to Washington, D.C. Their stay in the nation's capital, however, would be brief. War clouds loomed on the horizon.

Chapter 3

WAR HERO AND STATESMAN

By 1846, Davis's first year in Congress, ill will was growing between the United States and Mexico. The conflict had begun ten years earlier, in 1836. That year, Texas, a possession of Mexico with a large population of Americans, had declared itself an independent republic. Soon thereafter, Texas sought U.S. statehood. Mexico, however, did not recognize Texas's independence and warned the U.S. not to admit Texas to the Union. When the U.S. ignored the warning and made Texas a state in 1845, Mexico viewed this as an act of war. Mexico also disputed Texas's claim to territory between the Nueces River and the Rio Grande. Attempts to settle these disagreements peacefully failed, and war broke out in 1846.

OPPOSITE: Future president Zachary Taylor (center) led U.S. forces at the Battle of Buena Vista during the Mexican-American War.

Essentially, the conflict between the U.S. and Mexico was the outgrowth of the confident American belief in "Manifest Destiny"—the idea that it was the nation's obvious (or "manifest") fate to expand westward to the Pacific Ocean. The fact that the land was already settled by Hispanic peoples and Native American tribes—and that part of it belonged to Mexico—was overlooked. Acting on the concept of Manifest Destiny meant, for example, removing Native Americans from their traditional lands so white Americans could settle there. In 1846, it also meant sending military forces to Mexico to force the government to accept borders that gave the U.S. more territory.

Southern slave owners were strong supporters of Manifest Destiny and of the war with Mexico. They believed that the survival of their culture and of slavery depended on extending slavery into new western territories. As those territories applied for statehood, they would balance the new non-slave (called Free Soil) states and allow the South to retain equal power with the North in the U.S. Senate.

The war had great public support. Those who opposed it, such as a young Illinois congressman named Abraham Lincoln, found themselves in the minority. Opponents of the war were viewed with suspicion, and their patriotism was doubted. Lincoln, for instance, was not elected to a second term after he questioned the reasons for going to war with Mexico.

Jefferson Davis

The Mississippi Volunteers

In 1846, the United States annexed the New Mexico territory.
★

Davis, like many in the South, supported the war. When fighting broke out in 1846, he volunteered to lead a regiment of Mississippi troops into action. His offer was accepted, and he resigned from Congress in June 1846, returning to his home state to raise a fighting force. This proved to be easier said than done, because the volunteers were largely untrained. They were not accustomed to military discipline and fighting strategy.

Over the summer, however, Davis got his regiment into fighting shape. They, in turn, came to admire and respect "Colonel" Davis. "If he should tell his men to jump into a cannon's mouth, they would think it right," wrote one volunteer.

In early September, the 900 men of Davis's 1st Mississippi Infantry Regiment set off for Mexico. Over the next ten months, Davis and his men battled bravely and helped to turn the tide in America's favor at several key battles.

In late September, Davis and his troops arrived to serve under the command of General Zachary Taylor—Davis's former father-in-law—at the Battle of Monterrey. By the time the Mississippi volunteers arrived, Mexican cannons had nearly wiped out three companies of American soldiers. Davis decided to use the smoke from the cannons to his advantage. He had his men move quickly under cover of the smoke to a point within one hundred yards of the Mexican fortifications.

35

Davis's regiment helped American forces avoid defeat during the Battle of Buena Vista in the war with Mexico.

Then, suddenly, Davis ordered his men to charge. The Mexicans were caught by surprise and retreated.

A few months later, at the town of Buena Vista, American troops came under fire from a larger force of Mexicans. Davis had his men form a defensive position shaped like the letter V. When the Mexicans pushed their attack toward the bottom of the V, the troops on the side opened up in a murderous crossfire. Although Davis was shot in the foot, the battle was over quickly.

★

In 1847, the *North Star*, an abolitionist newspaper, was started by Frederick Douglass.

★

Return to Washington, D.C.

Though the U.S. did not win the Mexican-American War until 1848, Davis returned to Mississippi in July 1847 to recover from the wound in his foot. Many officers in the U.S. forces who fought in Mexico achieved fame in later years—future Civil War generals Robert E. Lee, Ulysses S. Grant, Thomas "Stonewall" Jackson, James Longstreet, and William Sherman all saw action. Davis, however, achieved immediate fame from his participation in the war, primarily because he had been a member of Congress before leading a successful volunteer brigade.

Shortly after his return to Brierfield, Davis was appointed to replace a U.S. senator from Mississippi who had died. Davis held that seat for the next four years while a number of significant events led to deeper division in the United States.

37

In 1849, thousands of people set out for California in a quest for gold.

One of those events took place thousands of miles from the nation's capital in the territory of California, newly acquired from Mexico. In 1848, gold was discovered in the foothills of the Sierra Nevada mountains west of Sacramento. When word of the discovery reached the East Coast late that year, it set off one of the largest migrations of Americans in the nation's history. In 1849, more than 80,000 people, known as Forty-niners, made the long journey to the West Coast.

As the number of Americans in California grew larger by the week, the push for statehood began. In 1849, however, there were 15 slave states and

15 free states. As in the case of the Missouri Compromise thirty years before, it fell to Congress to solve the problems of balancing slave and free states.

In fact, the question of slavery arose not only in California, but in all of the lands acquired from Mexico after the war. One congressman, David Wilmot of Pennsylvania, proposed the Wilmot Proviso as a solution to the slavery problem. This law prohibited slavery in all territory acquired from Mexico. The Senate, led by Davis and John

David Wilmot proposed that the United States prohibit slavery in territory acquired from Mexico.

Calhoun of South Carolina, voted down the proviso several times. They insisted that, according to the Constitution, it was the duty of Congress to protect the right of Southerners to own property—meaning slaves—in any territory.

During the debates over the question of slavery in the new territories, Davis acquired a reputation as one of the Senate's most forceful and convincing speakers. He was not, however, a natural politician. He hated compromise and considered anyone who disagreed with his politics a personal enemy. "He was a regular bulldog when he formed a opinion, for he would never let go," said one of his staff members.

39

John C. Calhoun and Nullification

Few men in American history have served the government longer than John C. Calhoun of South Carolina. First elected to Congress in 1811, Calhoun also served as secretary of war, senator, and as vice president under both John Quincy Adams and Andrew Jackson. By 1850, when he died, Calhoun had served the U.S. government for thirty-nine years.

Even though Calhoun served the nation so long, he opposed a strong central government and was a fierce defender of states' rights. So fierce was his devotion to those rights that in his final years as a senator, he became Congress's strongest voice in support of the theory of nullification.

According to the theory, originally developed by Thomas Jefferson more than 50 years earlier, states had the right to nullify—ignore—any federal laws with which they disagreed. Calhoun based his support of the theory on Jefferson's writing and on his own understanding of the Tenth Amendment to the Constitution: "Powers not delegated to the United States . . . are delegated to the states."

Although Jefferson had never suggested it, the most extreme interpretation of nullification meant that a state could leave the Union if its differences with the federal government became too great. Calhoun first used the idea of nullification to oppose a federal tariff—tax on goods—that hurt the South Carolina economy.

John C. Calhoun was a strong believer in states' rights.

As the debate over slavery grew more heated in the United States, Calhoun used the theory in support of slavery, although he was not in favor of secession. Others who accepted the theory of nullification, however, used it to justify both slavery and a state's withdrawal from the Union.

Davis, like many other Southerners, idolized Calhoun. Davis's strong defense of states' rights and his powerful speeches in Congress earned him the nickname "The Calhoun of Mississippi." It was a title he carried proudly.

Long before he was elected president in 1848, Zachary Taylor was Davis's commander in the army.

In the presidential election of 1848, Davis's former commander and father-in-law, Zachary Taylor, was elected to office. Though Taylor had no political experience, he was a hero of the Mexican War, and thus a popular figure with most Americans. He also owned a large plantation with more than 300 slaves. Thus, Southern members of Congress had an ally in the Oval Office. Despite Southerners' confidence in their power in Washington D.C., however, change was looming. The election of 1848 was notable for the fact that a third party, the Free Soil party, nominated a presidential candidate and had 13 of its representatives elected to Congress. The so-called "Free Soilers" were the first national party to take an antislavery position. Twelve years later, as the Republican Party, they nominated Abraham Lincoln for president.

Led by Free Soilers and by antislavery sympathizers, the debate in Congress over whether to permit slavery in newly acquired territories raged throughout most of 1849. And at the front of the pro-slavery side was Davis. He was completely devoted to the unlimited expansion of slavery as well as the concept of states' rights.

42

As 1850 arrived, pro-slavery and antislavery forces each realized that they had no real chance at complete victory. Finally, the Senate agreed on the Compromise of 1850. Under this compromise, California was admitted to the Union as a free state. In addition, both New Mexico and Utah were organized as territories. They would be admitted to the Union as either free or slave states, based on the constitution approved by their citizens—a concept known as "popular sovereignty." As a concession to antislavery groups, slave trade was prohibited in the District of Columbia, but slavery was not abolished there. Finally, a strict Fugitive Slave Law was enacted to protect the rights of Southern slave owners. Under this measure, law enforcement officials and private citizens anywhere in the United States were required to pursue any runaway slaves and return them to their owners. Until that point, slaves who escaped into Northern states were relatively safe from recapture.

In many ways, the Compromise of 1850 worsened the tensions between those on opposite sides of the slavery question. For antislavery Northerners, the Fugitive Slave Law was a bitter pill to swallow. Not only did the law require them to help capture runaway slaves, but anyone who helped an escaped slave could be arrested and prosecuted. Outraged, antislavery activists formed numerous secret groups that aided slaves who sought freedom in the North.

43

Senator Henry Clay (center) was a leading proponent of the Compromise of 1850.

A Short Return to Mississippi

For Davis, the bitterness in Congress over the slavery question, as well as the separation from his wife and family, led to his decision to resign his Senate seat and run for governor of Mississippi. He left Washington, D.C. in September 1851 to campaign for office in his home state. After losing that race in November, Davis happily returned to private life as a successful plantation owner at Brierfield.

Contentment, however, did not last long. In 1852, Davis's longtime friend and former congressional colleague, Franklin Pierce, was elected president. Pierce remembered Davis's successes in the war with Mexico, and offered his old friend the position of secretary of war—a cabinet position known today as secretary of defense.

Franklin Pierce (pictured) offered Davis the position of secretary of war.

At first, Davis was not sure he wanted the job. He did not want to leave his home state to spend time in the bitter political squabbles in Washington. A sense of duty, however, won out, and Davis accepted Pierce's offer.

46

Slave catchers used dogs to help track down runaway slaves.

Davis became one of the most efficient and imaginative men ever to hold the position of secretary of war. His first step was to increase the size of the army from 14,000 men to more than 18,000. He felt that with the expansion of the Union into territory occupied by Native Americans, troops would be needed to protect settlers. To make the armed forces more attractive to young men, Davis convinced Congress to approve the first pay raise for soldiers in more than forty years. He also won approval for increases in military pensions and benefits for the widows and orphaned children of soldiers killed in the service of their country.

Davis also brought many improvements to the army's weapons. All soldiers were issued rifled muskets—guns with grooves cut into the barrel that increased distance and accuracy. He also adopted a new type of bullet from France called the minié ball. This was a cone-shaped projectile made of soft lead that flattened on impact. Later, the use of rifled guns and minié balls during the Civil War caused enormous numbers of casualties on both sides.

As secretary of war, Davis also supervised the Corps of Engineers—an army unit that did construction work on all federal property, including the capitol. During Davis's term as secretary, the U.S. capitol was expanded and an aqueduct was built to bring fresh water from the Potomac River to Washington, D.C.

Not all of Davis's ideas were accepted. He brought camels to the United States from Turkey and Egypt. These animals were adapted to hot weather, and moved faster and needed less water than horses. Davis believed they would be useful in the deserts of the Southwest. Although they were effective, the ill-tempered "ships of the desert" were disliked by troops and were never used after Davis left office.

Secession and War

Davis's term as secretary of war ended when Pierce left office in 1857. Davis was still popular with voters in Mississippi, however, and the state legislature elected him to the U.S. Senate. He returned to a governing body that was even more divided than it had been six years earlier. Much of that division resulted from legislation passed by Congress in 1854: The Kansas-Nebraska Act.

In 1854, while Davis was the secretary of war, Senator David Atchison of Missouri sponsored a bill that divided the huge Nebraska territory into two territories, Kansas and Nebraska. Atchison and other lawmakers

Senator David Atchison of Missouri sponsored the Kansas-Nebraska Act.

49

"Bleeding Kansas" and John Brown

The passage of the Kansas-Nebraska Act had tragic consequences in the new territory of Kansas. Those consequences in turn propelled a fiery abolitionist named John Brown into national prominence.

Even before the act was signed into law, Northern abolitionists and Southern pro-slavery advocates each sent settlers into Kansas. Both sides were determined to influence the vote that would decide whether Kansas would be a slave state or free.

John Brown

On the day of the vote, March 30, 1855, more than 5,000 supporters of slavery rode into Kansas from Missouri. These "Border Ruffians" intended to achieve their aims by any means. They intimidated voters and stuffed the ballot boxes with illegal ballots. When the results were tallied, Kansas had apparently voted in favor of slavery.

Outraged abolitionists, however, declared the vote a fraud. Later in 1855, they met in Topeka, where they proclaimed the pro-slavery Kansas legislature illegal and drew up a constitution that called for Kansas to be admitted to the Union as a free state.

Tensions between the two sides soon erupted into violence. On May 21, 1856, hundreds of Border Ruffians sacked the antislavery stronghold of Lawrence, Kansas. They destroyed several homes, a hotel, and printing presses.

This enraged John Brown, one of the nation's most zealous abolitionists. On the night of May 24, Brown led a raid on slavery supporters in Pottowatamie, Kansas, in which five men were massacred. In revenge, pro-slavery activists again rampaged through Lawrence, killing one man. The violence escalated quickly, and the territory soon became known as "Bleeding Kansas."

As a result of his actions in Kansas, Brown became a national figure, viewed by many antislavery activists as a hero. He went east, where he was praised and honored in the press and was showered with countless invitations to dinners and social events.

Brown, however, was not in the East merely to socialize—he was seeking support for a new plan to combat slavery. He envisioned himself as the leader of a great uprising of slaves against their masters. The first step would be to seize the town of Harpers Ferry, Virginia (now West Virginia) and acquire weapons from the federal armory and arsenal located there. It took months to finalize the plan, but at last John Brown was ready. On October 16, 1859, Brown, along with a band of sixteen whites and five African Americans, launched the attack on the town.

The action proved disastrous. The raiders easily took over the armory and arsenal, but once there, they had no escape plan. The townspeople of Harpers Ferry fought the raiders until the military arrived on October 17 and surrounded Brown and his men. When Brown refused to surrender, U.S. Marines—led by Robert E. Lee—stormed the arsenal. Some of the raiders were killed; others, including Brown himself, were captured.

John Brown was brought to trial on November 2, 1859. He was found guilty and sentenced to death. He was executed on December 2.

This engraving depicts the capture of John Brown at Harpers Ferry in 1859.

believed that this would permit the two
regions to enter the Union as two states—
one slave and one free. Both territories,
however, were located north of the
southern border of Missouri. The Missouri
Compromise, passed more than thirty years
earlier, banned slavery in any territories north of
that line.

Northern lawmakers and abolitionists wanted
to uphold the Missouri Compromise. The South,
however, wanted the Missouri Compromise
overruled. Southern lawmakers realized that
unless the compromise was overturned, slave
states would gradually be outnumbered by free
states because most new territory in the growing
nation was north of Missouri's southern border.
Eventually, the balance of power would shift, they
felt, and slavery would be prohibited.

The debate over the Kansas-Nebraska Act was at
a standstill until an amendment was added that
was taken from the Compromise of 1850. The
amendment allowed the question of slavery to be
decided by "popular sovereignty"—a vote of the
residents in the territory—rather than the federal
government. As a senator for the second time,
Davis strongly supported states' rights as well as
the idea of popular sovereignty as a way to
determine whether a territory would be slave
or free.

The Kansas-Nebraska Act, signed into law in
May 1854, was a huge victory for the South.
Northerners, on the other hand, felt betrayed by

the government. Many threw their support behind a new political party, the Republican Party, formed from the Free Soil party and others with strong abolitionist views.

By 1860, the division between the North and South had reached the breaking point. The presidential election that year became a contest between pro-slavery and antislavery parties. The antislavery Republican Party nominated Abraham Lincoln of Illinois. The Democrats, however, split between a Northern candidate, Stephen Douglas—also from Illinois—and a Southern candidate, John Breckinridge of South Carolina. In addition, a pro-slavery third party nominated a candidate. Davis worked hard behind the scenes to convince the three pro-slavery candidates to support one nominee. He was un-successful, however, and Lincoln won the election with less than 40 percent of the popular vote.

Stephen Douglas (above) and John Breckinridge (below) both ran for president as Democrats in 1860.

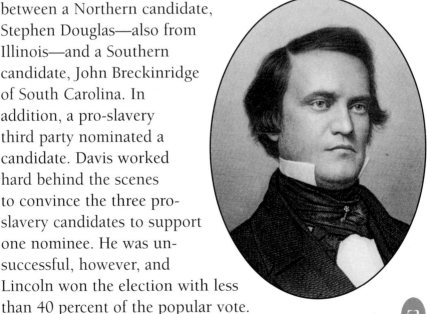

53

Lincoln had run on a party platform that promised to prohibit slavery in any new territories and to work for the abolition of slavery in states where it existed. His election was the turning point for the South. In December 1860, South Carolina became the first state to secede from the Union. Six more Southern states, including Mississippi, followed early in 1861.

On January 21 of that year, Davis took the Senate floor to give his farewell speech. Referring to language used by Thomas Jefferson in the Declaration of Independence, Davis said, "No man was born—to use the language of Mr. Jefferson—booted and spurred to ride over the rest of Mankind. Men were created equal— meaning . . . that there was no divine right to rule; that no man inherited the right to govern."

Davis also referred to the U.S. Constitution's position on African Americans: "There we find provision made for that very class of persons as property; they were not put upon the footing of equality with white men . . . but so far as representation was concerned, were discriminated against as a lower caste, only to be represented in the numerical proportion of three fifths."

Finally, Davis concluded with a message that, although secession meant breaking up the country, there was no need for bitterness. "I am sure I feel no hostility to you, Senators from the North. I am sure there is not one of you, whatever sharp discussion there may have been between us, to whom I cannot now say, in the presence of my God, I wish you well; and such, I am sure, is the feeling of the people whom I represent towards those whom you represent. I therefore feel that I but express their desire when I say I hope, and they hope, for peaceful relations with you, though we must part."

Those "peaceful relations" ended less than three months later. On April 12, 1861, Confederate artillery bombarded Fort Sumter in the harbor of Charleston, South Carolina. The Civil War had begun.

Chapter 4

"SURPRISED AND DISAPPOINTED"

A month after leaving Washington, D.C., Davis was tending the garden at his home in Mississippi. Suddenly, he looked up to see a man on horseback galloping toward the plantation. The rider halted in front of Davis and handed him a telegram that read:

> *"We are directed to inform you that you are this day unanimously elected President of the Provisional Government of the Confederate States of America and to request that you come to Montgomery [Alabama] immediately."*

OPPOSITE: Jefferson Davis was inaugurated as president of the Confederacy on the steps of the state capitol in Montgomery, Alabama.

57

Jefferson Davis was elected president of the Confederate States of America in 1861.

Davis had been elected by representatives from states that had seceded. These representatives had gathered in Montgomery in early February—before the fighting began at Fort Sumter. Davis was honored by his election, but he had not expected to serve the Confederacy in a political role. Because of his years of military experience and his term as secretary of war, he would have preferred to command the Confederate army. Years later, Davis recalled his reaction to the news of his election: "I was surprised, and still more, disappointed."

★
President Abraham Lincoln called for 75,000 men to volunteer to join the Union army in April 1861.
★

Although his farewell to Congress several weeks before had been peaceful, Davis felt sure that a war with the Union was rapidly approaching. Because of his time in Washington and in the North, he knew that the Confederacy faced a difficult task. The South, with 11 states and 9 million people—more than one-third of them slaves—would be at war with a Union of 23 states and a population of 22 million people. In addition, the South had little manufacturing capability and few reliable means of transportation. "We are without machinery, without means, and threatened by a powerful opposition," Davis wrote in a letter, "but I do not despond, and will not shrink from the task imposed on me."

Davis, accompanied by his wife and children, soon left Brierfield for Montgomery. On February 18, 1861, three weeks before Abraham Lincoln took the oath of office as the sixteenth president of the United States, Jefferson Davis stood on the

59

Jefferson Davis and his family moved into the first White House of the Confederacy in Montgomery.

steps of the capitol building in Montgomery. A band played "Dixie," then Davis was sworn in as the first president of the Confederate States of America. "It is joyous, in the midst of perilous times, to look around upon a people united in heart," he said in his inaugural address. He concluded the address with the statement that "We may hopefully look forward to success."

The Difficulty of Governing

Despite Davis's hopeful words, the reality of governing the Confederacy was much different. His forceful personality was not adapted to leading a nation whose constitution made him more of a figurehead than a true leader. The same men who had chosen Davis as president had also written a constitution that, in almost every respect, gave states greater powers than the central government.

Davis, who had been a military officer and a cabinet member, was used to having total control in most decisions. Thus, he found his new position difficult from the beginning. He clashed with members of his cabinet by requiring reports on the smallest details of their day-to-day work. Almost from the beginning of his term, he reversed decisions made by the war and state departments. The secretaries of those departments left within three months.

Davis, who had gained a reputation as a firm and uncompromising legislator in the Senate, angered many Southern lawmakers with his demeanor. He was often impatient and rude to colleagues. He also had great difficulty accepting any criticism and often took offense at the simplest comments or questions. "I wish I could learn just to let alone people who snap at me," Davis told his wife.

A little more than a month after the attack on Fort Sumter, the Confederate capital was moved

61

The Davis Family

★ ★ ★ ★ ★

As impatient and rude as he was in his political life, Jefferson Davis was a loving father who had a reputation for spoiling his children. Davis and Varina had six children: Samuel, Margaret, Jefferson Jr., Joseph, William, and Varina Anne. Davis brought his family with him to Richmond, and one visitor to the Confederate White House remarked, "Statesmen passing through the halls on their way to the discussion of weighty things were likely to hear the ringing laughter of the carefree and happy Davis children."

That happiness, however, did not last. Samuel died from an unknown disease as a child. Two weeks after his fifth birthday, Joseph died in an accident when he fell from the second floor porch of the Confederate White House. After the war, eleven-year-old William died from diphtheria. And Jefferson Jr. died from yellow fever at age twenty-one.

Both of Davis's daughters survived him. Varina Anne, however, died young from malaria. Margaret was the only Davis child to marry and have a family.

Jefferson and Varina Davis pose with their grandchildren.

The Confederate capital was moved to Richmond, Virginia, soon after the Civil War began.

to Richmond, Virginia, a city less than 100 miles from Washington, D.C. Davis and his family again moved, this time to the Confederate White House in Richmond. By now, Davis was fifty-four years old and in poor health from the effects of pneumonia and malaria earlier in his life. He suffered constant pain from the foot wound he had received in the Mexican War, earaches, eyesight damaged by the blinding snows in the north during his military service, and serious digestive problems. The demands of leading a new nation to war against an overwhelming opponent further weakened Davis over the next four years.

63

The Davis Administration

Serving in the administration of Jefferson Davis was a task as difficult as any in the Confederate government. Davis's tactless and irritable nature, along with his tendency to play favorites, earned him few allies. In fact, during the four-year history of the Confederacy, he appointed fourteen men to the seven cabinet positions. These men served with varying degrees of success.

Alexander Stephens. Stephens, from Georgia, served as vice president under Davis for four years. In public, he was a loyal Davis supporter and Confederate. In private, he felt that he was the better man to lead the Confederate government. He criticized Davis as "weak, timid, petulant, and obstinate."

Alexander Stephens

Judah Benjamin. Benjamin, from Louisiana, was a U.S. senator before the Civil War. In the Senate, he formed a close bond with Davis, and was Davis's only friend among his cabinet members. Benjamin, sometimes called "The Brains of the Confederacy," served initially as attorney general. Over the course of the war, he also served as secretary of war and secretary of state.

Judah Benjamin

Robert Toombs. Toombs, of Georgia, was Davis's first secretary of state. A strong-willed man who had served as a U.S. congressman and senator, he clashed almost immediately with

Davis, complaining that the president was constantly second-guessing and overruling his decisions. In fact, in early April 1861, when the Confederate cabinet met to decide whether or not to attack Fort Sumter, Toombs warned that "firing on Fort Sumter would inaugurate a civil war greater than any the world has ever seen." Toombs resigned after five months in the cabinet, because he believed he could render more valuable service on the battlefield.

Robert Toombs

Leroy P. Walker. Walker, of Alabama, was the first Confederate secretary of war, holding that post briefly from February to September 1861. In those seven months, Walker raised 200,000 troops and purchased arms and supplies. A rugged, tobacco-chewing lawyer, he resigned after Davis constantly questioned his management of the war department. Walker served as a general for the rest of the war.

Leroy P. Walker

James Seddon. Seddon was Davis's fourth and longest-serving secretary of war. Appointed in November 1862, Seddon held the position for so long because he was able to deal with Davis's overbearing personality. In the spring of 1863, Seddon opposed General Robert E. Lee's plan to invade the North. Lee, however, convinced Davis and other cabinet members to allow him to go ahead with the plan, against Seddon's wishes. The disastrous Battle of Gettysburg was the result. As the Confederacy fell, however, Seddon found himself, rather than Lee, being blamed for the failed strategy. Seddon resigned from office in February 1865.

James Seddon

The Battle of Bull Run was the Confederacy's first major victory in the Civil War.

Nevertheless, the initial months of the Civil War were encouraging for the Confederacy. The first major battle, in July, was fought less than fifty miles from Richmond at the railroad junction of Manassas, Virginia. Union and Confederate forces met at a river called Bull Run that ran through the town, with the Rebels achieving a resounding victory. In the heat of this battle, with Confederates falling back from the Union onslaught, a company of Virginians, led by General Thomas Jackson, formed a defensive circle on high ground. Seeing the determined Rebels fighting back, a Confederate officer cried, "There stand Jackson's men like a stone wall. Rally behind the Virginians." It was this key moment that led to the first Confederate victory and gave Jackson his legendary nickname— Stonewall.

By the end of the daylong fight, Union troops had panicked and were in a disorganized retreat to Washington. Davis rode his horse to the front lines. Falling back into his military habits, he rode among the soldiers and urged them to chase the Union forces and destroy them before they reached Washington. The long day's fighting in blistering heat, however, had exhausted the Rebel troops. To Davis's disgust, the Confederate leaders did not pursue the Federals.

Congress passed the first income tax law in August 1861, in order to finance the war.

In many ways, the episode at Bull Run was an example of the difficulties Davis faced as president. Despite the fact that he was the head of the Confederate government, he had little real power. Each state in the Confederacy raised its own fighting forces. The state decided where the forces would fight and who would command them. Although he could appoint generals to various positions, Davis had little power over the troops that fought for the Confederacy.

Davis's habit of playing favorites among the generals also caused him to lose the respect of the leaders and the forces fighting under them. Although Davis praised and promoted excellent officers such as Robert E. Lee and Albert Sidney Johnston, he also publicly criticized other competent and respected officers such as P.G.T. Beauregard, the commander at Manassas, and James Longstreet, a brave general who fought in every major battle of the war. Even worse, Davis

67

Mary Chesnut: The Diarist of the Confederacy

Some of the information that has come down through the years about day-to-day life during the Civil War was compiled in a diary written by Mary Chesnut. Born Mary Boykin Miller in Camden, South Carolina, she married James Chesnut in 1840. When James was elected to the Senate in 1858, Mary moved with him to Washington, where she became close friends with Varina and Jefferson Davis. When the Civil War began, James Chesnut served as aide to Davis.

Mary Chesnut

From February 1861 to July 1865, Mary Chesnut recorded her experiences both in Richmond and in the other cities she visited during the war. Those entries were published in 1905 as *A Diary from Dixie*. Portions of the diary describe Chesnut's interactions with the Davises.

Soon after Chesnut moved to the first Confederate capital of Montgomery, Alabama, she wrote:

> Lunched at Mrs. Davis's; everything nice to eat, and I was ravenous. For a fortnight I have not even gone to the dinner table. Yesterday I was forced to dine on cold asparagus and blackberries, so repulsive in aspect was the other food they sent me. Mrs. Davis was as nice as the luncheon. When she is in the mood, I do not know so pleasant a person. She is awfully clever, always.

Chesnut describes a conversation with Jefferson Davis just before the first large-scale battle of the war, at Bull Run:

> In Mrs. Davis's drawing-room last night, the President took a seat by me on the sofa where I sat. He talked for nearly an hour. After his experience of the fighting qualities of Southerners in Mexico, he believes that we will do all that can be done by pluck and muscle, endurance, and dogged courage, dash, and red-hot patriotism. And yet there was a sad refrain running through it all. For one thing, either way, he thinks it will be a long war. That floored me. It has been too long for me already. Then he said, before the end came we would have many a bitter experience. He said only fools doubted the courage of the Yankees.

Chesnut describes the accidental death of the Davises' five-year-old son in 1864:

> Poor little Joe, the good child of the family, was so gentle and affectionate. He used to run in to say his prayers at his father's knee. Now he was laid out somewhere above us, crushed and killed. Mrs. Semmes, describing the accident, said he fell from the high north piazza upon a brick pavement. Before I left the house I saw him lying there, white and beautiful as an angel, covered with flowers.

supported weak leaders who were despised by their men, such as Braxton Bragg, whose loss at Chattanooga in 1863 opened the way for the Union invasion of the South.

A Loss of Public Support

By early 1862, the South had won a number of decisive battles over the poorly led Federal troops. The losses on both sides, however, were terribly high, and most people now believed that the war would be long and bloody. Two key battles that year, one in the West and one in the East, underlined the awful toll the war would take.

Albert Sidney Johnston led Rebel troops at the Battle of Shiloh.

In early April, Confederate forces in Tennessee under General Albert Sidney Johnston surprised Union forces under General Ulysses Grant at Shiloh on the banks of the Tennessee River. The first day's fighting pushed the Union forces back considerably. That night, however, Federal reinforcements arrived and the next day, Union troops defeated the Rebels.

Shiloh was the first major Union victory. Johnston, one of Davis's favorite generals, was killed. Alarming to people on both

Davis rode among Rebel troops at Bull Run, urging them to pursue the retreating Federal forces.

The Battle of Shiloh was the first major Union victory of the Civil War.

sides was the huge toll—nearly 18,000 dead, wounded, and missing from both sides.

The following September, General Robert E. Lee, who had taken command of Confederate forces a few months earlier, launched the first Rebel invasion of the North. Directing his army into southern Maryland, he hoped to keep the fighting away from Virginia's Shenandoah Valley during harvest time. Lee also hoped that a Rebel victory on Northern soil would persuade foreign powers to recognize the Confederacy and offer military aid.

Early on September 17, 1862, fighting broke out between Rebels and Federals in the small farming town of Sharpsburg, Maryland, near Antietam Creek. By noon, ten thousand men lay dead and wounded. By nightfall, almost 23,000 men from both sides were dead, wounded, or missing. The battle of Sharpsburg, or Antietam, ended in basically a draw, with the Union gaining perhaps a mile of ground. It is remembered today as the bloodiest day in American military history.

Draw or not, the battle brought enormous changes to the war. Immediately after the fighting ended, President Lincoln issued the Emancipation Proclamation, freeing all slaves in the rebellious states. That move kept England and France from supporting the Confederacy, and Southern hopes for aid from those countries faded.

By the end of 1862, Davis's popularity began to fall in the South. Some newspapers criticized his strategy of fighting a defensive war by defending Southern territory, claiming it would invite Union invasion and lead to ruin. Yet when

Confederate soldiers lie dead after the Battle of Antietam, the bloodiest day in American military history.

On January 1, 1863, the Emancipation Proclamation went into effect.

★

he approved Lee's invasion of the North, other papers criticized his decision to fight an offensive war, pointing out that the Confederacy did not have the capability of carrying a war to the much larger enemy.

Davis also lacked political support. Because the Confederacy had no political parties, there was no organized legislative group to support the president. Most supported only the interests of their home states. Davis used his veto power to try to stop legislation more than thirty-five times. Yet each time, the legislation was passed over his veto. (By contrast, Lincoln used his veto only three times during the Civil War. He was able to control legislation because he had strong Republican support in Congress.)

By 1863, the Confederate treasury was almost out of money. Davis's recommendation to raise funds through higher taxes was ignored. The Confederacy sold bonds—IOUs—to investors, but they soon became worthless because the central government was too weak to raise money from the states to pay them off.

Troop shortages began to affect the South as the war dragged on. To increase the number of Confederate troops, Davis ordered the first military draft in history. The draft, however, pulled men away from their farms and left no one to tend the crops. As a result, food became scarce, and Southern citizens soon faced gnawing hunger. Riots broke out in Richmond, Atlanta, and other cities, as poor residents stormed the military supply depots. By 1863, the Confederate government was forced to use food supplies intended for troops to feed poor families.

By late spring 1863, Davis and many other Confederate leaders were desperate. Union forces in the West under General Ulysses S. Grant had surrounded Vicksburg, Mississippi—a city overlooking the Mississippi River only fifty miles from Jefferson's home at Brierfield. If Vicksburg fell, the Union would control the mighty Mississippi and the South would be split in two. Faced with this threat, Davis called Confederate commander Robert E. Lee to Richmond to discuss strategy.

Union leaders hoped to take control of Vicksburg, Missippi, in order to split the South in two.

THE CITY OF VICKSBURG, MISSISSIPPI, WHERE THE BATTERY WAS RAISED TO STOP PASSING VESSELS.-

75

Davis and other political leaders in Richmond wanted Lee to send half of his Army of Northern Virginia west to Mississippi to help break the siege of Vicksburg. Lee disagreed with the strategy. Instead, he supported another invasion of the North, this time into central Pennsylvania. A victory there would give the Rebels control of the Susquehanna River and enable them to cut rail supply lines to the west. From there, Lee planned to move east and bring the war to Philadelphia, Baltimore, and eventually, Washington, D.C. Lee believed that a successful Confederate attack into Pennsylvania would pull Grant's forces away from Vicksburg, thereby freeing that city from the siege.

In the end, Lee's plan won out. The general commanded such respect that the Confederate leaders followed his wishes, despite their misgivings after the disaster at Antietam.

Unfortunately for the South, Lee's strategy was a failure. Southern forces were defeated at the Battle of Gettysburg, the bloodiest battle in American military history. Over three days, July 1 to July 3, 1863, more than 50,000 Americans were killed and wounded in the small Pennsylvania town. Then, on July 4, the leaders in Richmond received word that Vicksburg had fallen to Grant, with 30,000 men taken prisoner. As an added insult, Federal troops had diverted to Davis's home, ransacked it, and freed his slaves. Although

These Confederate soldiers were taken prisoner after the Battle of Gettysburg.

the war continued for two more years with a number of Confederate victories, few Southerners truly believed the Confederacy could recover from the staggering losses at Gettysburg and Vicksburg.

Soon after the defeat at Gettysburg, Davis received a letter of resignation from General Lee. "No blame can be attached to the army for its failure to accept what was projected by me," Lee wrote. "Nor should it be censured for the unreasonable expectations of the public. I am alone to blame." Davis, knowing how beloved Lee was by his men, refused to accept the resignation.

Chapter 5

DEFEAT BECOMES INEVITABLE

In the spring of 1864, President Lincoln named General Ulysses S. Grant the commander of all Union armies. Grant sent his chief lieutenant general, William T. Sherman, across Georgia to capture Atlanta. Sherman's "March to the Sea" cut a 60-mile-wide path of destruction across the South and destroyed much the region's farmland, manufacturing facilities, and transportation. Meanwhile, Grant came east to join General William Meade's Army of the Potomac in an all-out attack on Richmond.

OPPOSITE: Ten months after the Battle of Cold Harbor, workers bury the dead. During the battle, more than 7,000 Union troops were killed in less than half an hour.

Grant's campaign began in May 1864, when the Army of the Potomac—more than 120,000 men—entered Virginia to take on Lee's force of just over 65,000 men. Over the course of next six months, battles were fought in the area known as the Wilderness in northern Virginia. Thousands of men fell in places such as Spotsylvania Court House and Cold Harbor. In most cases, Lee's men won the battles. At the Battle of Cold Harbor, more than 7,000 Union troops fell in less than thirty minutes—the highest rates of casualties in the entire war. Union troops there actually refused Grant's order to charge for a third time in the battle. Northern papers called Grant a butcher, but the tough cigar-chewing general would not pull back from his mission. His enormous force rolled on toward Richmond. The rapidly shrinking numbers of Confederate troops could only slow the Federals, not stop them.

Ulysses S. Grant

As the winter of 1864–1865 set in, Grant's men had forced the Confederates to Petersburg, a railroad town south of Richmond. Lee's Army of Northern Virginia, which now consisted of fewer than 35,000 men, dug miles of trenches around the rail center to protect the way to Richmond. This tattered force was all that stood between Federals and the Confederate capital. As he had at Vicksburg, Grant laid siege to Petersburg and planned to starve the Confederates over the long, cold winter.

In early 1865, Davis sent a delegation of Southerners to open negotiations with the North. Northern leaders wanted peace and were willing to allow emancipation to proceed at a rate slow enough to prevent the Southern economy from collapsing, but the Union refused to recognize the Confederacy as an independent nation. When he heard of the Union stance, Davis promised to keep fighting. Still believing that victory was possible, he persuaded the Confederate Congress to pass a bill that permitted slaves to enlist in the Confederate Army—and to grant any slave who did so his freedom.

By late March, more than 30,000 African Americans had enlisted in the Confederate army. But the manpower came too late. They were untrained and there were no weapons or food for them. In the miles of trenches around Petersburg and extending toward Richmond, Rebels endured the most horrible conditions imaginable. Starving and shoeless in tattered uniforms, the soldiers lived with rats, lice, and their own waste. The smell of their fallen comrades' decaying bodies filled the biting winter air.

Lee appealed numerous times to legislators in Richmond to allow his men to withdraw from their positions and head South to join the forces of General Joseph Johnston in North Carolina. This, of course, meant leaving Richmond undefended,

On February 1, 1865, Congress introduced the Thirteenth Amendment, which prohibited slavery.

Robert E. Lee grew increasingly frustrated with the Confederate congress.

so the congress refused to consider it. Lee grew angrier by the day as hundreds of his men deserted to return to their homes, and others simply died from hunger or disease at their entrenched posts. At one point Lee complained bitterly about the situation to his son Custis, an artillery commander, saying, "I have been up to see the congress and they don't seem to be able to do anything except eat peanuts and chew tobacco while my army is starving."

Finally, in late March 1865, Lee could stand no more. He rode directly to Davis's quarters in the Confederate White House. There he found Davis in his dining room studying maps. Lee told Davis that maintaining the trenches that defended Richmond was hopeless. He asked Davis's permission to withdraw southeast to join the force of General Joseph Johnston. There the troops could gather food and prepare to continue the fight. Davis knew that he had no choice. He told Lee to withdraw his forces and to "fight to the last."

Thus, in the last days of March 1865, General Lee made arrangements to withdraw his Army of Northern Virginia from the trenches in

A Spy in the Confederate White House?

When Jefferson Davis and his family moved into the Confederate White House in 1861, the staff of the home included an African American woman named Mary Elizabeth Bowser. Because she was an African American, most white people in Richmond assumed that Bowser was illiterate.

Bowser, however, had lived an unusual life for an African American in that time. Born in 1836, she worked in the plantation home of John Van Lew, serving his daughter, Elizabeth—who was a secret abolitionist. When Van Lew died in 1851, Elizabeth freed the family slaves. Since the slaves were treated fairly, however, Bowser chose to stay at the plantation and work for Elizabeth. In return, Elizabeth taught Bowser to read and write. She also arranged for Bowser to attend a Quaker school in Philadelphia for several years.

By 1861, Bowser was married and living in Richmond. At the outbreak of the war, Elizabeth Van Lew established a spy network for the Union and asked Bowser to join her. Bowser agreed, and Van Lew arranged a position for her at the Confederate White House. For four years, as she went about her household chores, Bowser kept alert for information. The information was passed on to Van Lew or to Thomas McNiven, a Richmond baker, who led the Union spy ring.

Little is known about Bowser's specific actions. After the war, Elizabeth Van Lew destroyed all of her correspondence with Bowser. Thomas McNiven's family destroyed his diary after his death. And in the 1950s, Bowser's family destroyed her diary. Nevertheless, in 1995, Mary Elizabeth Bowser was inducted into the United States Military Intelligence Corps Hall of Fame.

Petersburg, leaving Richmond defenseless. The troops were to march to the town of Amelia, two days west. There, Lee had made arrangements for supply trains to meet the army. The soldiers would eat, rest briefly, and travel on to meet the forces of Johnston in North Carolina. Lee was certain that even as weary and starved as they were, his men would continue to fight as long as they had life in their bodies.

Although Davis had consented to Lee's plan, the president did not realize that the withdrawal would happen so quickly. In fact, he learned of it while attending church services on Sunday morning, April 2. An aide handed him a note saying that Union forces were on the outskirts of the city, and that Lee's men were already on the move to the west. Davis immediately left church. Outside, he heard the distant roar of cannons. The capital was under attack.

Soon the entire city was in panic. As residents fled carrying their belongings on their backs, the streets were mobbed with people, horses, wagons, carts, and even wheelbarrows.

The Confederate government also went into action. Railroad cars on the Danville line were packed with boxes of records and more than $500,000 in gold and silver. Each car in the train was labeled with its department name. One car was the "War Department," another the "Treasury," and so on. The entire Confederate government was

Union troops laid waste to Richmond as soon as Lee's forces gave up its defense.

contained on one shabby collection of railroad cars.

For his part, Davis packed up his office through most of the day of April 2. His wife and children had left the city for Charlotte, North Carolina, several days earlier. At about seven in the evening, Davis climbed aboard a wagon packed with boxes and headed to the Richmond train station.

The train depot was jammed with anxious Southerners who hoped to flee Richmond by rail before the dreaded Yankees arrived. Many were attempting to force their way onto the Danville train. One man who was trying to board the train was a slave trader with a group of fifty slaves in chains. A Rebel soldier blocked the man at the

85

A Firsthand Account of the War

Mary Chesnut's *A Diary from Dixie* gives a close-up view of the progress of the war in the South. Her writing reveals how the initial excitement over the war gave way to fear and despair.

In one of her first entries, Chesnut describes being in Charleston, South Carolina, for the first shots of the war:

> *I did not know that one could live such days of excitement. Some one called: "Come out! There is a crowd coming." A mob it was, indeed, but it was headed by Colonels Chesnut and Manning. The crowd was shouting and showing these two as messengers of good news. They were escorted to Beauregard's headquarters. Fort Sumter had surrendered! Those upon the housetops shouted to us "The fort is on fire."*

Later, Chesnut writes of the horror of war close to home.

> *When we read of the battles in India, in Italy, in the Crimea, what did we care? Only an interesting topic, like any other, to look for in the paper. Now you hear of a battle with a thrill and a shudder. It has come home to us; half the people that we know in the world are under the enemy's guns. A telegram reaches you, and you leave it on your lap.*

You are pale with fright. How many, many will this scrap of paper tell you have gone to their death?

Times become more difficult as the war drags on.

At the turnpike we stood on the sidewalk and saw ten thousand men march by. We had seen nothing like this before. Hitherto we had seen only regiments marching spick and span in their fresh, smart clothes, just from home and on their way to the army. Such rags and tags as we saw now. Nothing was like anything else. Most garments and arms were such as had been taken from the enemy. Such shoes as they had on. Such tin pans and pots as were tied to their waists, with bread or bacon stuck on the ends of their bayonets. Anything that could be spiked was bayoneted and held aloft.

Sherman's march through the South terrorizes the Confederacy.

The end has come. No doubt of the fact. Our army has so moved as to uncover Macon and Augusta. We are going to be wiped off the face of the earth. What is there to prevent Sherman taking General Lee. We have lost nearly all of our men, and we have no money. Our best and bravest are under the sod; we shall have to wait till another generation grows up. Here we stand, with our houses burning or about to be.

Finally, in April 1865, the war comes to an end.

Richmond has fallen and I have no heart to write about it. Grant broke through our lines and Sherman cut through them. Stoneman is this side of Danville. They are too many for us. Everything is lost Yankees were expected here every minute.

On April 5, 1865, Lincoln visited the former Confederate capital of Richmond to inspect the damage.

entrance to the train. There was no room for all of them, he explained firmly. With his bayonet drawn, the soldier forced the trader to free the slaves—worth $50,000— before allowing him on board.

Davis and his cabinet were finally packed and on the train at about nine in the evening. Davis waved to the frightened citizens as the train pulled out and headed west, a government on wheels. Within two days, Richmond was under Union control. For many on the Federal side, the war was as good as over. For Lee and his army, however, there was still hope.

That hope vanished on April 4 when the Rebels stumbled into the sleepy town of Amelia, Virginia, not far from the county seat of Appomattox Court House. Arriving in the rail yard, Lee saw the supply trains waiting. Here was food at last for his starving men. Lee ordered the boxcars opened. Inside, instead of food, were cannon shells and gunpowder. Not a single ration was in the train's load—no ham, no bacon, no cornmeal, no milk. There was nothing for his 35,000 exhausted troops to eat.

Somehow in the hectic hours before the retreat, orders had been mixed up. The wrong train had been sent to Amelia. Standing before his men, the greatest general of the Civil War was speechless, his face a picture of "intense agony." His shoulders sagged. His troops would not have the strength to march another 140 miles to North Carolina. They

Lee surrendered to Grant at Appomattox Court House, Virginia.

would not be able to hold off the Union forces
bearing down on them.

Now, it seemed to the gallant commander, the
war was indeed over. After a few brief attempts to
break out of the Union encirclement, Lee surrendered his Army of Northern Virginia to Grant at
Appomattox Court House on April 9.

Davis received word of Lee's surrender the next
day, while his train stood in Danville. Completely
unprepared for the news, Davis sank into a chair
and wept. Yet he gave in to his feelings for only a
moment, then rose from his seat and promised to
fight all the way to Mississippi if necessary. He
ordered that remaining units of the Confederate
Army should scatter into the wilderness and begin
fighting a guerilla war.

Soon, Davis and his government on wheels was
on the move again. For a week, the train traveled

farther south, to Charlotte, North Carolina, then on to South Carolina. By April 15, there was no railroad track left on which to travel. William Sherman's Union forces had destroyed most of the rail lines in their march across the South. Over the next few weeks, Davis, joined by his wife and his cabinet, traveled more than 300 miles on horseback, escorted by a band of Tennessee cavalrymen.

On April 19, Davis received word that Abraham Lincoln had been assassinated.

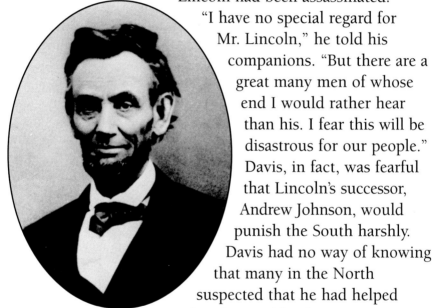

"I have no special regard for Mr. Lincoln," he told his companions. "But there are a great many men of whose end I would rather hear than his. I fear this will be disastrous for our people." Davis, in fact, was fearful that Lincoln's successor, Andrew Johnson, would punish the South harshly. Davis had no way of knowing that many in the North suspected that he had helped plan the president's assassination and that there was a $100,000 reward offered for his capture.

Abraham Lincoln was assassinated in April 1865.

As Davis continued south with his party, crowds greeted him warmly at every stop. He promised not to surrender as long as there were men willing to fight for the Confederate cause.

90

Then, on April 26, Davis learned that Joseph Johnston had surrendered his force in North Carolina. Word trickled in that many commanders had refused to obey Davis's orders to continue the war.

By May 2, most of Davis's cabinet had left to return to their homes. He met with his remaining cabinet and military aides one last time to convince them that if they could weather the next few weeks, the South would rally and fight back. But Davis was the only one who believed his words. His aides shook their heads. The South had suffered enough. It was nearly bled dry. It was time to give up. "Then all is lost," Davis said bitterly.

A little more than a week later, Union troops captured Jefferson Davis near Irwinville, Georgia. The Civil War was over now for the Confederate president, a month after the fall of Richmond and General Lee's surrender.

Chapter 6

THE FINAL YEARS

Immediately after his capture, Davis was taken to the seaport city of Savannah, Georgia. There, he was placed aboard a Union gunboat and transported north to Fort Monroe, Virginia, a military prison. For the first few weeks in prison, Davis had a ball and chain attached to his leg. Authorities removed the shackles after public protests, but Davis's treatment remained harsh.

OPPOSITE: Jefferson Davis (seated) spent more than two years in prison after the Civil War.

For three months, Davis was not allowed any contact with his wife or children. A soldier was stationed in his cell at all times, and a squad marched outside his door around the clock. The light in his cell was never allowed to go out. This severe treatment worsened Davis's health, and he never fully recovered from his time behind bars.

Varina Davis was finally allowed to see her husband on May 3, 1866, nearly a year after his capture. Alarmed at Davis's poor physical and mental condition, she began to seek support for his release. She wrote to Northern political leaders who supported healing the nation's wounds rather than punishing the Confederacy. Davis remained in prison for another year, until May 13, 1867. He was finally released on a bond of $100,000 that was provided by his supporters in both the North and South, including the influential New York newspaper publisher Horace Greeley.

Newspaper publisher Horace Greeley helped raise bond money for Davis's release from prison.

By the time of Davis's release, political events in Washington had led to bitter divisions between President Andrew Johnson and the so-called Radical Republicans in Congress. These divisions caused such turmoil in government that Davis became a forgotten man. Soon after his release,

94

Davis and his family left the United States and traveled to Europe and Canada, living on funds given by supporters.

★
In 1877, Thomas Edison patented the phonograph, or record player.
★

By the time the Davises returned to the United States in 1869, Ulysses S. Grant had been elected president, and he had no desire to punish any of the Confederate leaders. As a result, the U.S. government never brought Davis to trial on any charge.

Businessman and Author

In late 1869, Davis was offered a position as the president of a life insurance company in North Carolina. He took the job, but the company did not do well under his guidance. It went out of business in 1875, and Davis was near bankruptcy.

At that time, the Mississippi legislature offered to appoint Davis to his old position as U.S. senator. Knowing that he would have to request a federal pardon to serve in the Senate, Davis declined the offer. He simply did not feel that he had done anything wrong. He believed that he would dishonor his role as president of the Confederacy by requesting forgiveness from the federal government.

Davis's principles cost his family the security of a good salary. The plantation at Brierfield was in ruins, and, for a time, there was concern that the family would have nowhere to live. In 1877, however, a wealthy supporter of Davis's named Sarah Dorsey rented a cottage to the family on the

95

Jefferson Davis and his family lived in Beauvoir, an estate in Biloxi, Mississippi.

grounds of her home in Biloxi, Mississippi. Called "Beauvoir," (beautiful view" in French), the estate was located on the Gulf of Mexico. As soon as he settled in at Beauvoir, Davis began work on a book titled *The Rise and Fall of the Confederate Government*. The book was published in 1881 and became a best-seller.

Shortly before Davis's book was published, Dorsey died. In her will, she left the entire Beauvoir estate to Davis. Thus, the Confederate president and his family had a home for his final years.

Davis spent those years traveling through the South and making occasional speeches to veteran's groups. Although he believed that all Southerners should support the government of the United States, he never apologized for his actions and never requested that the American citizenship he lost as a Confederate officeholder be restored.

★
Abolitionist Frederick Douglass died in 1895.
★

On December 6, 1889, while on a trip to New Orleans, Louisiana, Davis died from pneumonia. His funeral drew a crowd of more than 200,000. It was the largest funeral for any American until President John Kennedy's in 1963. Davis was buried in New Orleans until 1893, when his body was taken to Hollywood Cemetery in Richmond, Virginia, where a statue honoring him stands over his grave.

In the years after her husband's death, Varina Davis worked to keep her husband's memory alive. She signed her name "Varina Jefferson Davis" and wrote a best-selling book about her life with her famous husband. In 1903, she sold Beauvoir to the United Sons of Confederate Veterans to be used as a soldier's home. More than 2,000 veterans lived there, and more than 700 are buried in the Beauvoir Confederate Cemetery. Varina Davis moved to New York City to live with her youngest daughter, and died in 1906.

Jefferson Davis was a month away from his eighty-second birthday when he died. In his long

The Daughter of the Confederacy

Although Jefferson Davis loved all of his children, his youngest child, daughter Varina Anne, became his favorite. Varina Anne, known as "Winnie," was born on June 27, 1864, only nine months before Richmond fell to the Union. After the war, she was the only one of Davis's children that he would allow to visit him in his dreary cell in Fort Monroe, Virginia. Because she was just a toddler, he felt that Winnie would be less affected by his situation than the older children.

An exceptional student, Winnie was educated in France during her high school years. In 1881, she returned to Beauvoir in Mississippi to be with her parents. A talented singer, painter, and writer, she spent long hours with her father, walking on the beach or playing cards with him. Winnie also accompanied Davis when he traveled to speaking commitments throughout the South. The slim, graceful young woman was loved by veteran's groups and became known as the "Daughter of the Confederacy."

Public affection, however, hurt Winnie Davis's private life. In 1888, she became engaged to attorney Alfred Wilkenson, a Northerner and the grandson of a well-known abolitionist. The Davises received threatening letters after the engagement was announced. Winnie was so upset by the furor that she left for an extended trip to Europe. It was there in late 1889

Varina Anne Davis, nicknamed "Winnie," was Jefferson Davis's youngest and favorite child.

that she received word of her father's death. Feeling it was her duty to carry on in her father's place as spokesperson for the Southern cause, she broke off her engagement and never married.

Winnie Davis spent her last years with her mother in New York City. She was the author of two novels and wrote numerous magazine and newspaper articles. In 1898, while attending a veteran's reunion, she contracted malaria and died at age 34.

life he was an army officer, a congressman, a war hero, a senator, and a cabinet member. His term as president of the Confederacy lasted for slightly more than four years. Yet it is for those four years—the most dramatic and tragic years in our nation's history—that Jefferson Davis is remembered today. In 1978, President Jimmy Carter signed a congressional resolution that officially restored citizenship to Davis, whom one senator called "an outstanding American."

Glossary

abolish To put an end to.

aqueduct A structure or canal built for carrying large quantities of flowing water.

cavalry An army on horseback.

cotton gin A machine that separates the seeds, hulls, and foreign materials from cotton.

emancipation Freedom.

inaugural Relating to a newly elected president's induction into office.

plantation An agricultural estate.

popular sovereignty The right of a state to decide whether or not to allow slavery.

regiment A military unit smaller than a brigade or a division.

secede To break away.

siege To take over.

strategy A plan.

veto The power a president has to say no to a piece of legislation.

For More Information

Books

Burch, Joan J. *Jefferson Davis: President of the Confederacy*
(Historical American Biographies). Berkeley Heights, NJ:
Enslow Publishers, 1998.

Frazier, Joey. *Jefferson Davis: Confederate President* (Famous
Figures of the Civil War Era). Broomall, PA: Chelsea House,
2001.

Gunderson, Corey Gideon. *Jefferson Davis* (Let Freedom Ring:
Civil War Biographies). Mankato, MN: Bridgestone Books,
2002.

Web Sites

Jefferson Davis
www.jeffersondavis.net

This comprehensive web site has biographical information, letters written by Davis, and links to other sites.

The Papers of Jefferson Davis
www.ruf.rice.edu/~pjdavis

Letters, documents, and speeches of Jefferson Davis, as well as
biographical information, are featured on this web site.

Jefferson Davis Biography
www.civilwarhome.com/davisbio.htm

This biographical web site offers links to Civil War biography
and overview web pages.

Index

Jefferson Davis